CHOCOLATE

CHOCOLATE

A BOOK OF RECIPES

HELEN SUDELL

LORENZ BOOKS

This edition is published by Lorenz Books,
an imprint of Anness Publishing Limited,
Blaby Road, Wigston, Leicestershire LE18 4SE; info@anness.com

www.lorenzbooks.com; www.annesspublishing.com

If you like the images in this book and would like to investigate
using them for publishing, promotions or advertising, please visit
our website www.practicalpictures.com for more information

A CIP catalogue record for this book is available from
The British Library

Publisher Joanna Lorenz
Editorial Director Helen Sudell
Designer Nigel Partridge
Illustrations Anna Koska

Photographers Gus Filgate, Nickey Dowey, Martin Brigdale,
Steven Wheeler, James Duncan, William Lingwood
Jacket photography Janine Hosegood
Recipes by: Catherine Atkinson, Joanna Farrow, Sara Lewis,
Claire Ptak, Suzanna Vandyck, Christine France, Mowie Kay, Ewa
Michalik, Maxine Clark, Georginal Campbell, Hannah Miles

COOK'S NOTES

• Bracketed terms are intended for American readers.

• For all recipes, quantities are given in both metric and imperial
measures and, where appropriate, in standard cups and spoons.
Follow one set of measures, but not a mixture, because they are
not interchangeable.

• Standard spoon and cup measures are level. 1 tsp = 5ml,
1 tbsp = 15ml, 1 cup = 250ml/8fl oz.

• Australian standard tablespoons are 20ml. Australian readers
should use 3 tsp in place of 1 tbsp for measuring small quantities.

• American pints are 16fl oz/2 cups. American readers should use
20fl oz/2.5 cups in place of 1 pint when measuring liquids.

• Electric oven temperatures in this book are for conventional
ovens. When using a fan oven, the temperature will probably
need to be reduced by about 10–20°C/20–40°F. Since ovens
vary, you should check with your manufacturer's instruction
book for guidance.

• The nutritional analysis given for each recipe is calculated per
portion (i.e. serving or item), unless otherwise stated. If the recipe
gives a range, such as Serves 4–6, then the nutritional analysis will
be for the smaller portion size, i.e. 6 servings. The analysis does not
include optional ingredients, such as salt added to taste.

• Medium (US large) eggs are used unless otherwise stated.

PUBLISHER'S NOTE

CONTENTS

INTRODUCTION

One of the greatest treasures ever discovered was the bean from the tree *Theobroma cacao*, the original source of chocolate. Smooth in texture, intense in taste, and subtly perfumed, chocolate is a rich source of sensory pleasure, adored by almost everyone who has tasted it. Divine it

Below: There is nothing more tempting than a delicious-looking slice of chocolate cake.

really is – the name Theobroma is a Greek word meaning "food of the gods". The ultimate decadent treat, it is hardly surprising that in the past chocolate has been credited with being an aphrodisiac. Chocolates are traditional lovers' gifts, and special events, such as Valentine's Day, Easter and Christmas, are celebrated with boxes of chocolates, chocolate eggs or the classic yuletide log.

Above: Chocolate truffles are easy to make and are wonderful to receive as a stylish gift.

Once the preserve of Aztec emperors, highly prized and coveted, chocolate was unknown in Europe until the middle of the 16th century, when it was introduced as a rare and wonderful beverage. It took almost 200 years before the sweetened chocolate bar made its appearance, and the rest, as they say, is history. Although chocolate is now

Right: There are many ways to serve chocolate as an elegant dinner party dessert.

accessible to all, familiarity has done nothing to dim its huge popularity. Consumption of all types of chocolate continues to rise. In recent years there has been an increased demand for the pure product with more than 50 per cent cocoa solids, and aficionados scout out new varieties of chocolate with all the enthusiasm and energy of the ardent wine buff.

For the cook, the fascination with chocolate goes even deeper. It is a sensitive ingredient that needs careful handling, but which offers remarkable rewards. The velvety texture and rich flavour add a touch of luxury to numerous cakes, cookies, puddings and desserts, and it is equally good in hot or cold dishes. As an added bonus, chocolate can be piped, shaped and moulded to make a variety of exciting decorations.

This book is for chocolate lovers everywhere. The brief introduction provides information on the different types of chocolate available and how they are used in cooking. Then there are step-by-step instructions explaining basic chocolate techniques – melting chocolate over water, tempering chocolate, marbling and feathering chocolate, and making decorations such as chocolate curls, shapes and leaves. For the recipe section, we've included classics like

Black Forest Gâteau and Chocolate Roulade. Also in the luscious line-up are Midnight Chocolate Chip Cookies, Chocolate and Date Whoopie pies with creamy centres, gloriously gooey puddings, voluptuous gâteaux and sweet chocolate treats for gifts and after-dinner delights. There's a recipe for a warming Hot Chocolate drink and even a White Chocolate Castle for a very special dessert. So go on, indulge yourself with this irresistible selection of recipes.

TYPES OF CHOCOLATE

Various types of chocolate are suitable for different recipes. It is important to use the right sort of chocolate for the best results possible. The quality of block chocolate varies according to the quantity of cocoa butter it contains. Most types have around 27 per cent. The higher the proportion of cocoa butter, the more easily it melts.

COCOA POWDER

This is the residue left after the cocoa butter has been pressed from the ground, roasted beans. Sweetened cocoa is used for drinks. It can also be blended with powdered milk to become commercial 'drinking chocolate'. Unsweetened cocoa powder is used for baking.

COUVERTURE CHOCOLATE

Used by professional cooks because it melts smoothly, this has a high cocoa butter content (up to 70 per cent) but needs tempering. Also called dipping or coating chocolate, it comes in dark, milk and white options.

UNSWEETENED CHOCOLATE

This chocolate has no added sugar and a high proportion of cocoa butter. It is used mainly for baking. It is also called 'bitter', 'baking chocolate' or 'cooking chocolate'.

DARK (BITTERSWEET) CHOCOLATE

This chocolate is unsweetened chocolate to which less than a third of sugar has been added.

PLAIN (SEMISWEET) CHOCOLATE

This contains more sugar than dark chocolate and is often used for cooking. Many brands

print on the packaging the percentage of cocoa in the chocolate. The higher the percentage of cocoa, the less sweet the chocolate is.

MILK, SWEET OR EATING CHOCOLATE

Rarely used for cooking, this chocolate tastes good because of added sugar and condensed or powdered milk.

WHITE CHOCOLATE

This is creamy in colour and texture as it does not contain any cocoa solids but does contain cocoa butter and sugar. It does not set as firmly as milk and dark chocolate and is rarely used in baking. It is called 'white coating' in the US.

CHOCOLATE DROPS, STRANDS AND BUTTONS

Drops and buttons are used in baking, as part of a cake and also as decorations. Strands are sprinkled over iced cakes.

Cocoa powder

Dark (bittersweet) chocolate

White couverture chocolate

Plain chocolate drops

Milk couverture chocolate

Plain chocolate curls

White chocolate curls

White chocolate

Milk chocolate

Chocolate strands

Plain (semisweet) chocolate

Milk chocolate drops

Dark couverture chocolate

White chocolate drops

White chocolate buttons

COOKING WITH CHOCOLATE

MELTING CHOCOLATE OVER WATER

When melting chocolate for use in recipes, all equipment must be completely dry. Do not cover during or after melting because any water or condensation could cause the chocolate to seize or stiffen.

1 Chop the chocolate into small pieces. Put the chocolate in the top of a double boiler or in a heatproof bowl over a pan of barely simmering water. The bottom of the bowl should not touch the water.

2 Heat gently until the chocolate is melted and smooth, stirring occasionally. Remove from the heat and stir.

MELTING CHOCOLATE IN A MICROWAVE

Melting chocolate in a microwave is fast but it must be checked at 5–10-second intervals as the chocolate could quite easily burn. These times are for a 650–700W oven and are approximate, as microwave ovens vary.

1 Place 115g/4oz chopped or broken dark (bittersweet) or plain (semisweet) chocolate in a microwave-safe bowl and microwave on medium for about 2 minutes. The same quantity of milk or white chocolate should be melted on low for about 2 minutes.

2 Check the chocolate at 5–10 second intervals during the cooking time.. The chocolate will not change shape, but will start to look shiny. It must then be removed from the microwave and stirred until completely melted and smooth.

TEMPERING CHOCOLATE

When chocolate is tempered it is melted very carefully to a specific temperature, cooling it and reheating, so that the right kind of crystals predominate in the mixture, which gives it a glossy, smooth finish. The tempering process is used when chocolate is being melted to use as a decoration or finishing touch, for example coating little cakes or dipping fruit or nuts into chocolate. Without tempering, melted chocolate may well end up with a grainy or chalky finish.

Once it has been tempered properly, chocolate is much

Above: Tempered chocolate has a glossy, smooth appearance.

more resistant to higher temperatures later in the cooking process. Chocolate that has not been tempered correctly will not set properly and hardens very slowly at room temperature.

To temper light or dark chocolate successfully, you will need a marble slab or a similar cool, smooth surface and a chocolate thermometer.

1 Break up the chocolate into small pieces and place it in a heatproof bowl over a pan of hot water. Heat gently until completely melted.

2 Remove from the heat. Spoon about three-quarters of the melted chocolate on to a marble slab or other cool, smooth, non-porous work surface. With a plastic scraper or metal spatula, spread the chocolate thinly, then scoop it up before spreading it again. Repeat the sequence several times, keeping the chocolate constantly on the move, for about 5 minutes.

3 Using a chocolate thermometer, check the temperature of the chocolate as you work it. As soon as the temperature registers 28°C/82°F, tip the chocolate back into the bowl and stir into the remaining chocolate. With the addition of the hot chocolate, the temperature should now be 32°C/90°F, making the chocolate ready for use. To test, drop a little of the chocolate on to the marble; it should set very quickly.

FEATHERING OR MARBLING CHOCOLATE

These two related techniques provide some of the easiest ways of decorating the top of a cake or dessert but will still result in an impressive finish.

1 In separate heatproof bowls melt 2 contrasting colours of chocolate. Spread one of the chocolate colours over the cake to be decorated. Try to get a smooth, even finish.

2 Spoon the contrasting chocolate into a piping (pastry) bag and pipe lines or swirls over the chocolate base.

3 Using a skewer or cocktail stick (toothpick) draw through the lines or swirls in oppposite directions to create a feathered or marbled effect.

MAKING CHUNKY CHOCOLATE CURLS

If you want to make chunky curls, it is best to use chocolate that has been melted with pure white vegetable fat, which keeps it from hardening completely. The finished decorations are suitable for all kinds of cakes and desserts, and look even more striking if you use contrasting colours of white and dark chocolate.

1 Melt 175g/6oz plain (semisweet) or dark (bittersweet) chocolate with 30ml/2 tbsp pure white vegetable fat (shortening), stirring until smooth.

2 Pour the melted chocolate into a small rectangular tin (pan) lined with foil or baking parchment to produce a block about 2.5cm/1in thick. Chill until set.

Right: Chocolate curls can be used to decorate large cakes or sprinked over desserts.

3 Allow the block to come to room temperature, remove it from the tin and place on a clean piece of non-stick baking paper. Hold it with a piece of folded foil or paper towel (to stop it melting) and use a cheese slice to produce large curls. If you require short chunky curles then use a swivel-bladed peeler. The block can also be grated.

MAKING CHOCOLATE SCROLLS

Use chocolate as prepared for Chunky Chocolate Curls (left) to produce these long or cup-shaped scrolls.

1 Pour the chocolate evenly on to a marble slab or the back of a baking sheet. Using a metal spatula, spread to about 3mm/⅛in thick and allow to set for about 30 minutes, until just firm.

2 To make long scrolls, use the blade of a long, sharp knife on the surface of the chocolate, and, with both hands, push away from your body at a 25–45 degree angle to scrape off a thin layer of chocolate. Use a teaspoon to make cup-shaped curls.

COATING OR DIPPING IN CHOCOLATE

For recipes that require coating or dipping use tempered couverture (see page 10) chocolate for the best results. If couverture chocolate is difficult to find, use plain (semisweet) chocolate instead, but chill immediately to prevent a bloom forming on the surface.

1 Melt the chocolate then pour it into a small bowl for dipping. The temperature should be about 46°C/115°F.

2 Use two forks to lower the truffle or fruit into the chocolate. Turn to coat thoroughly and lift out. Place the dipped candy or fruit on a non-stick baking sheet until dry. Chill immediately.

GRATING CHOCOLATE

Chocolate can be grated by hand or in a food processor. Make sure you grate it at a cool temperature.

1 Chill the chocolate and hold it with a piece of folded foil or paper towel to prevent the heat of your hand melting it. Hold a hand- or box-grater over a plate and grate with an even pressure.

2 A food processor fitted with the metal blade can also be used, but be sure the chocolate is soft enough to be pierced with a sharp knife. Cut the chocolate into small pieces and, with the machine running, drop the chocolate pieces through the feeder tube until very fine shavings are produced.

CHOPPING CHOCOLATE

It is best to use a heavy chef's knife to chop blocks of chocolate. If it is a very large block, break it into smaller pieces first.

1 Starting at one corner, chop the chocolate with a large, heavy knife, using your non-dominant hand to hold the tip of the knife down.

2 Once you have chopped all the way along, turn the board 90° and repeat until all the chocolate is chopped finely.

SPECIAL OCCASION AND SMALL CAKES

TRIPLE-CHOCOLATE MACARONS, WHOOPIE PIES,

GORGEOUS GÂTEAUX WITH CREAMY FILLINGS,

AND EXTRAVAGANT CAKES WITH INDULGENT

ICING MAKE MEMORABLE CHOCOLATE CREATIONS

FOR ANY SPECIAL OCCASION

CHOCOLATE TRUFFLE MUFFINS

Not an everyday muffin, these luscious chocolate treats with a hidden truffle centre, and equally sinful soft chocolate frosting, are decorated with pretty seashell chocolates.

Makes 9

165g/5½oz/scant ¾ cup butter, softened
150g/5oz/⅔ cup light muscovado (brown) sugar
3 eggs, lightly beaten
150g/5oz/1¼ cup self-raising (self-rising) flour
25g/1oz/¼ cup unsweetened cocoa powder
7.5ml/1½ tsp baking powder

For the truffles

150g/5oz dark (bittersweet) chocolate, broken into pieces
20ml/4 tsp double (heavy) cream

For the frosting

250ml/8fl oz/1 cup double (heavy) cream
75g/3oz/⅓ cup soft light brown sugar
5ml/1 tsp vanilla extract
150g/5oz dark (bittersweet) chocolate, grated
chocolate seashells, to decorate

Preheat the oven to 180°C/350°F/Gas 4. Line the cups of a muffin tin (pan) with paper cases. To make the truffles, melt the chocolate in a heatproof bowl set over a pan of simmering water. Remove from the heat, and stir in the cream. Set aside to cool and thicken. Scoop the cool mixture into 9 balls.

To make the muffins, beat the butter and sugar in a bowl. Beat in the eggs. Sift in the flour, cocoa and baking powder and mix lightly. Half fill the paper cases. Add a truffle to the centre of each. Spoon the remaining cake batter on top. Bake for 22–25 minutes. Cool.

For the frosting, put the cream, sugar and vanilla in a pan and heat until it reaches boiling point. Remove from the heat. Stir in the chocolate until melted. Cool. Spread on top of cold muffins and decorate with chocolate seashells.

Energy 331kcal/1381kJ; Protein 3.6g; Carbohydrate 28.6g, of which sugars 27.4g; Fat 23.5g, of which saturates 14.3g; Cholesterol 110mg; Calcium 32mg; Fibre 0.3g; Sodium 191mg.

CHOCOLATE DATE WHOOPIE PIES

These unusual whoopie pies are for those with a really sweet tooth. Fluffy chocolate cakes with chunks of chewy dates are sandwiched together by a sticky dulce de leche filling.

Makes 12

125g/4¼oz/8½ tbsp unsalted (sweet) butter, softened
175g/6oz/¾ cup light muscovado (brown) sugar
seeds of 1 vanilla pod (bean)
1 egg
300g/11oz/2¾ cup plain (all-purpose) flour
50g/2oz unsweetened cocoa powder
7.5ml/1½ tsp bicarbonate of soda (baking soda)
5ml/1 tsp salt
75g/3oz/½ cup dates, stoned (pitted) and chopped
250ml/8fl oz/1 cup buttermilk
200g/7oz dulce de leche
icing (confectioners') sugar, for dusting

Energy 327kcal/1384kJ; Protein 5g;
Carbohydrate 57g, of which sugars 37g;
Fat 11g, of which saturates 7g;
Cholesterol 45mg; Calcium 78mg;
Fibre 0.9g; Sodium 379mg.

Preheat the oven to 180°C/350°F/Gas 4. Line two baking trays with baking parchment or silicone mats. Whisk the butter, sugar and vanilla seeds until light and fluffy. Add the egg and whisk well.

In a separate bowl, sift the flour with the cocoa powder, bicarbonate of soda and salt, then stir in the dates.

Fold the flour mixture into the butter mixture in three stages, alternating each addition with the buttermilk, until all of the flour mixture and the buttermilk have been incorporated.

Using a piping (pastry) bag fitted with a large plain nozzle, pipe 24 5cm/2in rounds of cake mixture (batter) 5cm/2in apart on each baking tray. Bake for 12–15 minutes, or until the cakes bounce back when pressed. Transfer to a wire rack and leave to cool completely.

Spread a tablespoonful of dulce de leche on to the flat side of one cake and cover with the flat side of another. Repeat to make 12 pies. Dust with sifted icing sugar.

TRIPLE CHOCOLATE MACARONS

A rich chocolatey classic macaron, these are by far the easiest to make. Chocolate macaron shells are filled with a chocolate ganache, then decorated with a sprinkle of cocoa powder, if you like.

Makes 16

60g/2¼ oz egg whites
60g/2¼ oz/generous ¼ cup
   caster (superfine) sugar
7.5ml/1½ tsp egg white powder
120g/4¼ oz/generous cup icing
   (confectioners') sugar
50g/2 oz/ ground almonds
10g/¼ oz/½ cup unsweetened
   cocoa powder, plus extra for
   sprinkling, if liked

For the filling

75g/3oz dark (bittersweet)
   chocolate
60ml/4 tbsp single (light) cream

Line a baking tray with baking parchment. Fit a piping (pastry) bag with a plain round tip.

Place the egg whites in a clean bowl, and sift the caster sugar and egg white powder over the egg whites. Whisk with an electric whisk until stiff peaks form.

In a separate bowl, sift together the icing sugar, ground almonds and cocoa powder. Add the egg white mixture to the almond mixture. Using a spatula, gently fold the mixture until the batter falls in ribbons when lifted with the spatula.

Fill the piping bag with the mixture and pipe 24 4cm/1½in rounds onto the lined baking tray. Preheat the oven to 130°C/250°F/ Gas ½, and leave the baking tray out in a warm, dry room for at least 15 minutes.

Place the tray in the middle of the oven and bake for 10 minutes. Remove from the oven and allow to cool.

For the filling, melt the chocolate with the cream in a non-stick pan and heat over a low heat, stirring, until well combined. Remove from the heat and allow to cool, stirring occasionally, until thickened.

Place a teaspoon of chocolate ganache onto the flat side of one macaron shell, and top with the flat side of another macaron shell. Repeat to make 12 macarons. Sprinkle the tops of the macarons with cocoa powder, if you like.

Energy 91kcal/393kJ; Protein 2.4g; Carbohydrate 9.7g, of which sugars 9.4g; Fat 5.1g, of which saturates 1.8g; Cholesterol 2.7mg; Calcium 18mg; Fibre 0.6g; Sodium 30mg

SACHERTORTE

This glorious gâteau was created in Vienna in 1832 by Franz Sacher, a royal chef. It is filled with apricot jam and then sumptuously covered with rich chocolate icing and decorative curls.

Serves 10–12

225g/8oz dark (bittersweet) chocolate, broken into squares

150g/5oz/10 tbsp unsalted (sweet) butter, softened

115g/4oz/generous ½ cup caster (superfine) sugar

8 eggs, separated

115g/4oz/1 cup plain (all-purpose) flour

chocolate curls, to decorate

For the glaze

225g/8oz/¾ cup apricot jam

15ml/1 tbsp lemon juice

For the icing

225g/8oz plain dark (bittersweet) chocolate, broken into squares

200g/7oz/1 cup caster (superfine) sugar

15ml/1 tbsp golden (light corn) syrup

250ml/8fl oz/1 cup double (heavy) cream

Preheat the oven to 180°C/350°F/Gas 4. Grease a 23cm/9in round springform tin (pan). Line with baking parchment. Melt the chocolate in a heatproof bowl over a pan of hot water.

Cream the butter and sugar in a bowl until pale and fluffy. Add the egg yolks, one at a time, beating after each addition. Beat in the melted chocolate. Sift the flour over the mixture and fold in.

Whisk the egg whites until stiff, then stir a quarter into the chocolate mixture to lighten it. Fold in the remaining whites. Turn the mixture into the cake tin and smooth level. Bake for 50–55 minutes, or until firm. Turn out on to a wire rack to cool.

Heat the apricot jam with the lemon juice in a small pan until melted, then strain. Slice the cake horizontally into two even layers. Brush the cut surfaces and sides of each layer with the apricot glaze, then sandwich together. Place on a wire rack.

Mix the icing ingredients in a heavy pan. Heat gently, stirring until thick. Simmer for 3–4 minutes, without stirring, until the mixture registers 95°C/200°F on a sugar thermometer. Pour over the cake and spread evenly. Decorate with the curls and leave to set before serving.

Energy 625kcal/2618kJ; Protein 7.6g; Carbohydrate 73.1g, of which sugars 65.5g; Fat 35.8g, of which saturates 20.8g; Cholesterol 184mg; Calcium 73mg; Fibre 1.2g; Sodium 143mg.

CHOCOLATE AND ALMOND CAKE

This rich chocolate cake is filled with a sweet almond paste and then topped with a thick layer of chocolate icing. Perfect to serve at tea-time or as a satisfying dessert.

Serves 6

6 eggs, separated
115g/4oz/1 cup caster
   (superfine) sugar
150g/5oz/1¼ cups
   unsweetened cocoa powder
150g/5oz/1¼ cups ground
   almonds

For the almond paste

150g/5oz/1¼ cups caster
   (superfine) sugar
120ml/4fl oz/½ cup water
150g/5oz/1¼ cups ground
   almonds
15–30ml/1–2 tbsp lemon juice
½ vanilla pod (bean)

For the icing

115g/4oz dark (bittersweet)
   chocolate, chopped
25g/1oz/2 tbsp unsalted
   (sweet) butter, cubed
120ml/4fl oz/½ cup double
   (heavy) cream
50g/2oz/½ cup icing
   (confectioners') sugar, sifted

Preheat the oven to 200°C/400°F/Gas 6. Grease and line a 20cm/8in springform cake tin (pan). Beat the egg yolks in a large bowl, add the sugar and beat until the mixture is thick and creamy. Add the cocoa powder and almonds, and gently fold in.

Whisk the egg whites until stiff peaks form. Fold a spoonful of the whites into the yolk mixture, then mix in the remaining whites. Spoon into the tin and bake for 1 hour, or until a skewer inserted into the centre comes out clean. Cool in the tin.

Make the almond paste. Gently heat the sugar and water in a pan until the sugar has dissolved. Boil for 5 minutes, or until a thick syrup forms. Stir in the almonds and transfer to a bowl. Add the lemon juice and the seeds from the vanilla pod. Mix well.

Remove the cake from the tin and slice into two even layers. Sandwich the two halves together with the almond paste.

Make the icing. Melt the chocolate and butter in a heatproof bowl over a pan of simmering water. Remove from the heat and stir in the cream, then add the sugar and stir well. Cover the top of the cake with the chocolate icing. Leave to set.

Energy 892kcal/3726kJ; Protein 23g; Carbohydrate 73.7g, of which sugars 69.3g; Fat 58.4g, of which saturates 19g; Cholesterol 228mg; Calcium 226mg; Fibre 7.2g; Sodium 349mg.

HAZELNUT AND CHOCOLATE CAKE

A deliciously rich and nutty cake, perfect for those indulgent moments. It is a compact cake and can be sliced in the traditional way or cut into squares for the occasional lunchbox treat.

Serves 8–10

115g/4oz/½ cup unsalted
   (sweet) butter, softened, plus
   extra for greasing
150g/5oz plain (semisweet)
   chocolate, finely chopped
115g/4oz/generous ½ cup
   caster (superfine) sugar
4 eggs, separated
115g/4oz/1 cup ground
   hazelnuts, lightly toasted
50g/2oz/1 cup breadcrumbs
grated rind of 1½ oranges
30ml/2 tbsp strained
   marmalade, warmed
60ml/4 tbsp chopped
   hazelnuts, to decorate

For the icing

150g/5oz plain (semisweet)
   chocolate, finely chopped
50g/2oz/¼ cup unsalted
   (sweet) butter, diced

Energy 490kcal/2040kJ; Protein 7.2g;
Carbohydrate 38.2g, of which sugars 33.8g;
Fat 35.4g, of which saturates 15.1g;
Cholesterol 113mg; Calcium 62mg;
Fibre 2g; Sodium 172mg.

Preheat the oven to 180°C/350°F/Gas 4. Butter a 23cm/9in round cake tin (pan) and line the base of the tin with a sheet of baking parchment.

Melt the plain chocolate in a heatproof bowl over a pan of simmering water, stirring occasionally. Set aside when completely melted.

Beat the butter and sugar together, then gradually add the egg yolks, beating well. The mixture may curdle slightly. Beat in the melted chocolate, then the hazelnuts, breadcrumbs and orange rind. Whisk the egg whites until stiff, then fold into the chocolate mixture. Transfer to the cake tin. Bake for 40–45 minutes, until set. Remove from the oven, Allow to stand for 5 minutes, then transfer to a wire rack until cold.

To make the icing, place the chocolate and butter in a heatproof bowl over a pan of simmering water and stir until smooth. Leave until cool and thick.

Spread the cake with the marmalade, then the icing. Sprinkle over the nuts, then leave to set.

CLASSIC CHOCOLATE ROULADE

This rich, squidgy chocolate roll should be made at least eight hours before serving to allow it to soften. Expect the roulade to crack a little when you roll it up.

Serves 8

200g/7oz plain (semisweet) chocolate, broken into squares
200g/7oz/1 cup caster (superfine) sugar, plus extra caster or icing (confectioners') sugar to dust
7 eggs, separated
300ml/½ pint/1¼ cups double (heavy) cream

Preheat the oven to 180°C/350°F/Gas 4. Grease a 33 x 23cm/13 x 9in Swiss roll tin (jelly roll pan) and line the tin with baking parchment.

Melt the chocolate in a heatproof bowl over a pan of simmering water. Remove from the heat and leave to cool for about 5 minutes.

In a large bowl, whisk the sugar and egg yolks until light and fluffy. Stir in the melted chocolate. Whisk the egg whites until stiff, but not dry, and then gently fold into the chocolate mixture.

Pour the chocolate mixture into the prepared tin, spreading it level with a metal spatula. Bake for about 25 minutes, or until firm. Leave the cake in the tin and cover with a cooling rack. Cover the rack with a damp dish towel, then wrap in clear film (plastic wrap). Leave in a cool place for 8 hours, preferably overnight.

Dust a sheet of baking parchment with caster or icing sugar and turn out the roulade on to it. Peel off the lining paper. Whip the cream until soft peaks form and spread it evenly over the roulade. Roll up the cake from a short end. Dust generously with more sugar before serving.

Energy 476kcal/1988kJ; Protein 7.4g;
Carbohydrate 42.6g, of which sugars 42.4g;
Fat 32g, of which saturates 18.1g;
Cholesterol 219mg; Calcium 65mg;
Fibre 0.6g; Sodium 73mg.

BLACK FOREST GÂTEAU

Perhaps the most famous chocolate cake of all, this Kirsch-flavoured gâteau is layered with fresh cream containing chopped black cherries. It is perfect for a special occasion.

Serves 10–12

75g/3oz/6 tbsp unsalted (sweet) butter, melted, plus extra for greasing
5 eggs
175g/6oz/scant 1 cup caster (superfine) sugar
50g/2oz/½ cup plain (all-purpose) flour, sifted
50g/2oz/½ cup unsweetened cocoa powder, sifted

For the filling and topping

75–90ml/5–6 tbsp Kirsch
600ml/1 pint/2½ cups double (heavy) cream
425g/15oz can black cherries, drained, pitted and chopped

For the decoration

225g/8oz plain (semisweet) chocolate, to make chocolate curls, see page 12
15–20 fresh cherries, preferably with stems
sifted icing (confectioners') sugar (optional)

Preheat the oven to 180°C/350°F/Gas 4. Grease and line two 20cm/8in round deep cake tins (pans) with baking parchment.

Put the eggs and sugar in a large bowl and beat with an electric whisk for about 10 minutes, or until the mixture is thick and pale and leaves a trail when the beaters are lifted.

Sift together the flour and cocoa powder, then sift again into the whisked mixture. Fold in gently using a metal spoon and a figure-of-eight motion. Slowly trickle in the cooled melted butter and fold in gently.

Divide the batter between the tins and smooth level. Bake for 30 minutes, until springy to the touch. Leave in the tin for 5 minutes, then turn out on to a wire rack to cool. Peel off the lining paper.

Cut each cake in half horizontally. Sprinkle the four layers evenly with the Kirsch.

In a large bowl, whip the cream until it holds soft peaks. Transfer two-thirds of the cream to another bowl and stir in the chopped cherries.

Place a layer of cake on a serving plate and spread over one-third of the filling. Top with another portion of cake and continue layering, finishing with the cake top.

Use the remaining whipped cream to cover the top and sides of the gâteau. Decorate with chocolate curls, cherries and a dusting of icing sugar.

Energy 448kcal/1864kJ; Protein 4.8g; Carbohydrate 26.4g, of which sugars 22.7g; Fat 35.2g, of which saturates 21.1g; Cholesterol 161mg; Calcium 61.8mg; Fibre 0.8g; Sodium 121mg.

CHOCOLATE COOKIES, SLICES AND BARS

CRISP AND CRUNCHY COOKIES, GORGEOUS

BROWNIES, FABULOUS FRUITY FLORENTINES

AND LIGHT CHOCOLATE WHIRLS – TOTALLY

IRRESISTIBLE AND SATISFYING TREATS TO ENJOY

AT ANY TIME OF DAY

MIDNIGHT CHOCOLATE CHIP COOKIES

These cookies are so called because you can make them up before you go to bed and leave them to bake slowly in the switched-off oven. Hey presto – there they are in the morning!

Makes 9

1 egg white
90g/3½oz/½ cup caster (superfine) sugar
50g/2oz/½ cup ground almonds
90g/3½oz/generous ½ cup milk chocolate chips
90g/3½oz/scant ½ cup glacé (candied) cherries, chopped
50g/2oz/⅔ cup sweetened, shredded coconut

COOK'S TIP
Instead of leaving the cookies in the oven overnight you can put them in for about 6 hours during the day.

Energy 185kcal/777kJ; Protein 2.7g;
Carbohydrate 23.5g, of which sugars 23.4g;
Fat 9.6g, of which saturates 5g;
Cholesterol 2mg; Calcium 48mg;
Fibre 1.3g; Sodium 21mg.

Preheat the oven to 220°C/425°F/Gas 7. Line a baking sheet with baking parchment.

Put the egg white in a large, clean, grease-free bowl and whisk until stiff peaks form.

Add the caster sugar to the whisked egg white, a spoonful at a time, whisking well between each addition until the sugar is fully incorporated. The mixture should be completely smooth and glossy in appearance. Use an electric mixer for speed.

Fold in the almonds, chocolate chips, cherries and coconut, mixing until well combined. Place 9 spoonfuls of the mixture on the baking sheet, spacing them slightly apart.

Place in the oven, close the door then turn the oven off. Leave overnight and don't open the door. Serve the cookies for breakfast.

ROCKY ROAD CHOCOLATE BARS

This recipe is fun to make with children. They will love smashing the biscuits. Adults will also enjoy the contrast of melting chocolate chips, crunchy biscuits and soft marshmallows all blended together.

Makes 16

225g/8oz/1 cup salted butter
115g/4oz dark (bittersweet)
chocolate, roughly broken up
30ml/2 tbsp caster (superfine)
sugar
30ml/2 tbsp golden (light corn)
syrup
30ml/2 tbsp good quality
unsweetened cocoa powder
350g/12oz mixed digestive
biscuits (graham crackers)
and ginger nut biscuits
(gingersnaps)
50g/2oz mini marshmallows
75g/3oz mixed white and milk
chocolate chips
icing (confectioners') sugar,
for dusting (optional)

Energy 296kcal/1237kJ; Protein 2.7g;
Carbohydrate 28.6g, of which sugars 15.7g;
Fat 19.9g, of which saturates 11.6g;
Cholesterol 40mg; Calcium 39mg;
Fibre 0.9g; Sodium 245mg.

Line a 20cm/8in square cake pan, measuring about 2.5cm/1in deep, with baking parchment.

Put the butter in a pan with the chocolate, sugar, syrup and cocoa powder. Place over a gentle heat until completely melted.

Put the biscuits into a large plastic bag and smash with a rolling pin until broken up into rough chunks. Stir the biscuits into the chocolate mixture, followed by the marshmallows and chocolate chips. Mix together until everything is well coated in chocolate.

Spoon the mixture into the pan, but don't press down too much – it should look like a rocky road. Chill for at least 1 hour, or until firm.

Remove the cake from the pan and cut into 16 bars. If you like, dust the bars with icing sugar before serving.

CHOCOLATE FLORENTINES

These big, flat, crunchy cookies are just like traditional florentines but use tiny seeds instead of nuts.
Rolling the edges in milk or white chocolate makes them look like a real treat.

Makes 12

50g/2oz/¼ cup unsalted
  (sweet) butter
50g/2oz/¼ cup caster
  (superfine) sugar
15ml/1 tbsp milk
25g/1oz/scant ¼ cup
  pumpkin seeds
40g/1½oz/generous ¼ cup
  sunflower seeds
50g/2oz/scant ½ cup raisins
25g/1oz/2 tbsp multi-coloured
  glacé (candied) cherries,
  chopped
30ml/2 tbsp plain (all-purpose)
  flour
125g/4¼oz milk or white
  chocolate

Preheat the oven to 180°C/350°F/Gas 4. Line two baking sheets with baking parchment and grease the paper well. In a pan, melt the butter with the sugar, stirring, until the sugar has dissolved, then cook until bubbling. Remove the pan from the heat and stir in the milk, pumpkin and sunflower seeds, raisins, glacé cherries and flour. Mix well.

Using a teaspoon, spoon the mixture on to each baking sheet, spacing them well apart. Bake for 8–10 minutes. Using a metal spatula, push back the edges of the cookies to neaten. Leave on the baking sheets for about 5 minutes to firm up, then transfer to a wire rack to cool.

Break up the chocolate and put in a heatproof bowl set over a pan of gently simmering water. Heat, stirring frequently, until melted. Roll the edges of the cookies in the chocolate and leave to set on a clean sheet of baking parchment for about 1 hour.

Energy 157kcal/656kJ; Protein 2.2g;
Carbohydrate 17.5g, of which sugars 14.8g;
Fat 9.1g, of which saturates 4.3g;
Cholesterol 11mg; Calcium 40mg;
Fibre 0.6g; Sodium 38mg.

CHOCOLATE WHIRLS

These cookies are so easy that you don't even have to make any dough. They're made with ready-made puff pastry rolled up with a chocolate filling. They are very easy to eat too!

Makes about 20

75g/3oz/scant ½ cup golden caster (superfine) sugar
40g/1½oz/⅓ cup unsweetened cocoa powder
2 eggs
500g/1¼lb puff pastry
25g/1oz/2 tbsp butter, softened
75g/3oz/generous ½ cup sultanas (golden raisins)
90g/3½oz milk chocolate

Preheat the oven to 220°C/425°F/Gas 7. Lightly grease two sheets of baking parchment.

Put the sugar, cocoa powder and eggs in a large bowl and mix to a firm paste.

Roll out the pastry on a lightly floured surface to make a 30cm/12in square. Trim off any rough edges using a sharp knife.

Dot the pastry all over with the softened butter, then spread evenly with the chocolate paste and sprinkle the sultanas over the top.

Roll the pastry into a sausage-shape, then cut the roll into 1cm/½in slices. Place the slices on the baking sheets, spacing them apart.

Bake the cookies for 10 minutes, until risen and pale golden. Transfer to a wire rack and leave to cool.

Break the milk chocolate into small pieces and put in a heatproof bowl set over a pan of gently simmering water. Heat, stirring frequently, until melted and smooth.

Spoon or pipe lines of melted chocolate over the tops of the cookies, taking care not to completely hide the swirls of chocolate filling.

Energy 165kcal/689kJ; Protein 2.9g; Carbohydrate 18.6g, of which sugars 9.4g; Fat 9.5g, of which saturates 1.9g; Cholesterol 23mg; Calcium 34mg; Fibre 0.4g; Sodium 117mg.

COOK'S TIP
These pastries are not too sweet and are similar to Danish pastries, so you could even make them as a special treat for breakfast.

RICH CHOCOLATE BROWNIES

These brownies are packed with both milk and plain chocolate instead of adding sugar to the mixture. Serve them in small squares as they are very rich.

MAKES 16

300g/11oz each plain (semisweet) and milk chocolate
175g/6oz/¾ cup unsalted (sweet) butter
75g/3oz/⅔ cup self-raising (self-rising) flour
3 large (US extra large) eggs

> **COOK'S TIP**
> When buying plain (bittersweet) chocolate, bear in mind that the higher the percentage of cocoa solids, the higher the quality of the chocolate, and also the less sugar it contains. The best quality has 70 per cent cocoa solids.

Preheat the oven to 180°C/350°F/Gas 4. Line the base and sides of a 20cm/8in square cake tin (pan) with baking parchment.

Break the plain chocolate and 90g/3½ oz of the milk chocolate into pieces and put in a heatproof bowl with the butter. Melt over a pan of barely simmering water, stirring frequently.

Chop the remaining milk chocolate into chunky pieces. Stir the flour and eggs into the melted chocolate until evenly combined. Stir in half the chopped milk chocolate and turn the mixture into the prepared tin, spreading it into the corners. Sprinkle with the remaining chopped chocolate.

Bake the brownies for 30–35 minutes, until risen and just firm to the touch. Leave to cool in the tin, then cut the mixture into squares. Store the brownies in an airtight container.

Energy 213kcal/892kJ; Protein 4g; Carbohydrate 14g, of which sugars 11g; Fat 16g, of which saturates 10g; Cholesterol 77mg; Calcium 67mg; Fibre 0.3g; Sodium 100mg

CHOCOLATE WANDS

You need to work quickly making these cookies – it might take a few attempts to get the technique right. Bake only two at a time to make sure you have time to shape them into wands.

Makes 10–12

3 egg whites
90g/3½oz/½ cup caster (superfine) sugar
25g/1oz/2 tbsp unsalted (sweet) butter, melted
30ml/2 tbsp plain (all-purpose) flour
15ml/1 tbsp unsweetened cocoa powder
30ml/2 tbsp single (light) cream
90g/3½oz milk chocolate and multi-coloured sprinkles, to decorate

Preheat the oven to 180°C/350°F/Gas 4. Line two large baking sheets with baking parchment and grease the paper well. In a bowl, briefly beat together the egg whites and sugar until the whites are broken up. Add the melted butter, flour, cocoa powder and cream to the egg whites and beat until smooth.

Place two teaspoonfuls of the mixture to one side of a baking sheet and spread the mixture into an oval shape, about 15cm/6in long. Spoon more mixture on to the other side of the baking sheet and shape in the same way.

Bake for 7–8 minutes, until the edges begin to darken. Prepare two more cookies on the second baking sheet so you can put them in the oven while shaping the first batch.

Leave the cookies on the paper for 30 seconds, then lift one off and wrap it around the handle of a wooden spoon. Once it hardens, ease it off the spoon and shape the second cookie. Continue baking and shaping the cookies.

Break the chocolate into pieces and place in a heatproof bowl set over a pan of hot water, stirring until melted. Dip the ends of the cookies in the chocolate, until thickly coated. Sprinkle the chocolate-coated ends with coloured sprinkles and place on baking parchment. Leave for 1 hour until set.

Energy 103kcal/432kJ; Protein 1.6g;
Carbohydrate 14.3g, of which sugars 12.2g;
Fat 4.8g, of which saturates 2.9g;
Cholesterol 8mg; Calcium 28mg;
Fibre 0.3g; Sodium 41mg.

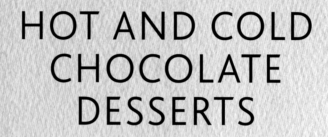

HOT AND COLD CHOCOLATE DESSERTS

RICH AND DARK, CREAMY WHITE, AND SIMPLE

MILK CHOCOLATE ALL MAKE DELICIOUS DESSERTS,

FROM HOT CHOCOLATE FONDUE AND PANCAKES

FULL OF FLAVOUR TO A BELGIAN CHOCOLATE

MOUSSE AND A CHILLED LAYERED TERRINE.

CHOCOLATE AND ORANGE SOUFFLÉ

The base in this hot soufflé is an easy-to-make semolina mixture, rather than the thick white sauce that many soufflés call for. If preferred replace a third of the orange juice with Grand Marnier.

Serves 4

butter, for greasing
600ml/1 pint/2½ cups milk
50g/2oz/generous ⅓ cup
*   semolina*
50g/2oz/scant ¼ cup light
*   muscovado (brown) sugar*
grated rind of 1 orange
90ml/6 tbsp fresh orange juice
3 eggs, separated
75g/3oz plain (semisweet)
*   chocolate, grated*
icing (confectioners') sugar,
*   for sprinkling*
single (light) cream, to serve

Preheat the oven to 200°C/400°F/Gas 6. Butter a shallow 1.75 litre/3 pint/7½ cup ovenproof dish.

Pour the milk into a heavy pan, sprinkle over the semolina and sugar, then heat, stirring the mixture constantly, until boiling and thickened.

Remove the pan from the heat, beat in the orange rind and juice, egg yolks and all but 15ml/1 tbsp of the grated plain chocolate.

Whisk the egg whites until stiff peaks form, then lightly fold one-third into the semolina mixture. Fold in another third, followed by the remaining egg whites. Spoon the mixture into the buttered dish and bake for about 30 minutes, until just set in the centre.

Sprinkle the soufflé with the reserved grated chocolate and the icing sugar, then serve immediately, with the cream handed around separately.

Energy 321kcal/1353kJ; Protein 12.2g;
Carbohydrate 43.7g, of which sugars 33.8g;
Fat 12.2g, of which saturates 5.9g;
Cholesterol 153mg; Calcium 219mg;
Fibre 0.8g; Sodium 123mg.

MAGIC CHOCOLATE MUD CAKE

Guaranteed to be a big hit, this scrumptious dessert can be put together in no time at all. When your guests break into the cake a delicious sauce 'magically' appears from beneath the sponge.

Serves 4

50g/2oz/¼ cup butter, plus extra for greasing
90g/3½oz/¾ cup self-raising (self-rising) flour
5ml/1 tsp ground cinnamon
75ml/5 tbsp unsweetened cocoa powder
200g/7oz/1 cup light muscovado (brown) or demerara (raw) sugar
475ml/16fl oz/2 cups milk
crème fraîche, Greek (US strained plain) yogurt or vanilla ice cream, to serve

Preheat the oven to 180°C/350°F/Gas 4. Grease a 1.5 litre/ 2½ pint/6¼ cup ovenproof dish with butter. Place the dish on a baking sheet and set aside.

Sift the flour and ground cinnamon into a bowl. Sift in 15ml/1 tbsp of the cocoa and mix well.

Place the butter in a pan. Add 115g/4oz/½ cup of the sugar and 150ml/¼ pint/⅔ cup of the milk. Heat gently without boiling, stirring from time to time, until the butter has melted and all the sugar has completely dissolved. Remove the pan from the heat.

Stir in the flour mixture, mixing evenly. Pour the mixture into the prepared dish and level the surface.

Mix the remaining sugar and cocoa in a bowl, then sprinkle over the pudding mixture. Pour the remaining milk evenly over the pudding.

Bake for 45–50 minutes or until the sponge has risen to the top and is firm to the touch. Serve hot, with crème fraîche, yogurt or ice cream.

Energy 480kcal/2025kJ; Protein 10g;
Carbohydrate 77.6g, of which sugars 58.3g;
Fat 16.7g, of which saturates 10.2g;
Cholesterol 34mg; Calcium 227mg;
Fibre 3g; Sodium 309mg.

BITTER CHOCOLATE FONDUE WITH POACHED PEARS

Pears and chocolate are a match made in heaven. Here, vanilla-scented poached pears are dipped into a rich chocolate fondue. The sprigs of rosemary add a herby flavour.

Serves 4–6

juice of 1 lemon
90g/3½oz/½ cup vanilla caster (superfine) sugar
1–2 fresh rosemary sprigs
12–18 small pears, or 4–6 large pears

For the fondue

200g/7oz dark (bittersweet) chocolate, broken into pieces
75ml/2½fl oz/⅓ cup strong black coffee
75g/3oz/scant ⅓ cup soft light brown sugar
120ml/4fl oz/½ cup double (heavy) cream

To poach the pears, put the lemon juice, sugar, rosemary sprigs and 300ml/½ pint/1¼ cups water in a pan large enough to accommodate the pears all in one layer. Bring to the boil, stirring until the sugar dissolves in the water.

Peel the pears, and halve the large ones, if using, but leave the stalks intact. Add to the hot syrup and spoon over to cover.

Cook for 5–10 minutes, depending on size and ripeness, spooning the syrup over them and turning frequently, until they are just tender. Transfer to a serving plate, then remove the rosemary sprigs from the syrup. Take the rosemary leaves off the stalks and discard the stalks. Stir about 15–30ml/1–2 tbsp of the rosemary leaves into the syrup and then leave to cool.

Put the chocolate in a heatproof bowl over a pan of barely simmering water. Add the coffee and sugar and heat, without stirring, until the chocolate is melted. Stir in the cream and heat gently. Transfer the fondue to a fondue pot and place on a burner set at a low heat at the table.

Serve the pears and syrup together with the hot chocolate fondue.

Energy 464kcal/1949kJ; Protein 2.8g; Carbohydrate 71.9g, of which sugars 71.6g; Fat 20.3g, of which saturates 12.3g; Cholesterol 29mg; Calcium 59mg; Fibre 5.6g; Sodium 15mg.

CHOCOLATE AMARETTO MARQUISE

This delightful dessert is bound to turn a few heads. It is infused with delicious amaretto liqueur, and can be made in a round tin if you don't have a heart-shaped one.

Serves 10 – 12

15ml/1 tbsp flavourless vegetable oil, such as groundnut (peanut) or sunflower
75g/3oz/7–8 amaretti, finely crushed
25g/1oz/¼ cup unblanched almonds, toasted and finely chopped
450g/1lb dark (bittersweet) or plain (semisweet) chocolate, chopped into small pieces
75ml/5 tbsp amaretto liqueur
75ml/5 tbsp golden (light corn) syrup
475ml/16fl oz/2 cups double (heavy) cream
unsweetened cocoa powder, for dusting

For the amaretto cream

350ml/12fl oz/1½ cups whipping cream or double (heavy) cream
30–45ml/2–3 tbsp Amaretto di Sarone liqueur

Lightly oil a 23cm/9in heart-shaped or springform cake tin (pan). Line the bottom with baking parchment and oil the paper. Combine the crushed amaretti and the chopped almonds. Sprinkle evenly on to the base of the tin.

Place the chocolate, amaretto liqueur and golden syrup in a pan over a very low heat. Stir frequently until the chocolate is melted and the mixture is smooth. Remove from the heat and allow to cool for about 6–8 minutes, until the mixture feels just warm to the touch.

Pour the cream into a bowl. Whip with a hand-held electric mixer, until it just begins to hold its shape. Stir a large spoonful into the chocolate mixture, to lighten it, then quickly add the remaining cream and gently fold into the chocolate mixture. Pour into the prepared tin, on top of the amaretti and almond mixture. Level the surface. Cover the tin and chill overnight.

To unmould, run a thin-bladed sharp knife under hot water and dry carefully. Run the knife around the edge of the tin to loosen the dessert. Place a serving plate over the tin, then invert to unmould. Carefully peel off the paper, replacing any crust that sticks to it, and dust with cocoa powder. In a bowl, whip the cream and amaretto liqueur to soft peaks. Serve separately.

Energy 589kcal/2444kJ; Protein 3.9g; Carbohydrate 38.2g, of which sugars 35.1g; Fat 46.4g, of which saturates 27.5g; Cholesterol 87mg; Calcium 63mg; Fibre 1.2g; Sodium 57mg.

MINIATURE CHOC ICES

For summer entertaining, these little chocolate-coated ice creams make a fun alternative to the more familiar after-dinner chocolates. Be creative with toppings and adapt them to suit the occasion.

Makes about 25

750ml/1¼ pints/3 cups vanilla,
    chocolate and coffee ice cream
200g/7oz plain (semisweet)
    chocolate, broken into
    small pieces
25g/1oz milk chocolate, broken
    into small pieces
25g/1oz/¼ cup chopped
    hazelnuts, lightly toasted

COOK'S TIP
If the melted plain
chocolate is very runny,
leave it for a few minutes
to thicken up slightly
before spooning it over the
ice cream scoops. The milk
chocolate can be piped on
the choc ices, using a bag
fitted with a writing nozzle.

Energy 117kcal/488kJ; Protein 1.8g;
Carbohydrate 10.7g, of which sugars 10.6g;
Fat 7.7g, of which saturates 4.3g;
Cholesterol 1mg; Calcium 36mg;
Fibre 0.3g; Sodium 19mg.

Put a baking sheet in the freezer for 15 minutes. Use a melon baller to scoop balls of each of the different ice cream flavours on to the baking sheet. Freeze for 1 hour until firm.

Line a second baking sheet with baking parchment and place in the freezer for 15 minutes. Melt the plain and milk chocolates in separate heatproof bowls set over a pan of simmering water.

Transfer the ice cream scoops to the paper-lined sheet. Spoon a little plain chocolate over a scoop so that most of it is coated. Sprinkle with chopped nuts, before the chocolate sets. Coat the remaining scoops with the dark chocolate. Sprinkle chopped nuts over half of the chocolate-covered scoops, working quickly.

Once the chocolate has set on the half that are not topped with nuts, drizzle each with milk chocolate. Freeze until ready to serve.

BELGIAN CHOCOLATE MOUSSE

Every Belgian family has its favourite recipe for this culinary classic, usually involving some combination of melted chocolate with fresh eggs and cream, butter, coffee and liqueur.

Serves 4

150g/5oz Callebaut callets (semi-sweet bits) or other good-quality Belgian chocolate, cut into small pieces

200ml/7fl oz/scant 1 cup whipping or double (heavy) cream

75g/3oz/6 tbsp caster (superfine) sugar

2 eggs, separated, at room temperature

chocolate curls or sprinkles, roasted almond slivers, strips of candied orange peel, unsweetened cocoa powder or extra whipped cream, to decorate (optional)

Put the chocolate in a heatproof bowl over a small pan of simmering water. Melt the chocolate, stirring occasionally. When it is smooth, scrape it into a large bowl and leave to cool to room temperature.

In a clean bowl, whip the cream with 15ml/1 tbsp of the sugar until it stands in soft peaks. Set aside.

In a separate, grease-free bowl, whisk the egg whites, gradually adding 50g/2oz/4 tbsp of the remaining sugar, until they from stiff peaks.

Whisk the egg yolks in a third bowl, gradually adding the last of the sugar, until foamy. Fold the yolks into the chocolate.

Using a spatula, fold in the whipped cream and then the egg whites. Spoon into ramekins or dessert glasses and leave to set for at least 4 hours. Serve plain or with any of the suggested decorations.

Energy 550kcal/2290kJ; Protein 5.9g;
Carbohydrate 44.3g, of which sugars 43.9g;
Fat 40.1g, of which saturates 23.8g;
Cholesterol 166mg; Calcium 61mg;
Fibre 1g; Sodium 50mg.

WHITE CHOCOLATE CASTLES WITH FRESH BERRIES

These romantic-looking chocolate cases serve a wide variety of uses. They can be frozen with iced mousses or filled with scoops of your favourite ice cream and succulent fresh berries.

Serves 6

225g/8oz white chocolate,
   broken into pieces
250ml/8fl oz/1 cup white
   chocolate ice cream
250ml/8fl oz/1 cup dark
   (bittersweet) chocolate ice
   cream
115g/4oz/1 cup blueberries and
   redcurrants
unsweetened cocoa powder,
   for dusting

Put the white chocolate in a heatproof bowl, set it over a pan of gently simmering water and leave until melted. Line a baking sheet with baking parchment. Cut out 6 30 x 13cm/12 x 5in strips of baking parchment, then fold each in half lengthways.

Stand a 7.5cm/3in pastry (cookie) cutter on the baking sheet. Roll one strip of paper into a circle and fit inside the cutter with the folded edge on the base paper. Stick the edges together with tape.

Remove the cutter and make more paper collars in the same way, leaving the cutter in place around the final collar.

Spoon a little of the melted chocolate into the base of the collar supported by the cutter. Using a teaspoon, spread the chocolate over the base and up the sides of the collar, making the top edge uneven. Carefully lift away the cutter.

Make 5 more chocolate cases in the same way, using the cutter for extra support each time. Leave the cases in a cool place or in the refrigerator to set.

Carefully peel the baking parchment from the sides of the chocolate cases, then lift the cases off the base. Transfer to serving plates. Using a teaspoon, scoop the ice creams into the cases and decorate with the fruit. Dust with cocoa powder.

Energy 351kcal/1463kJ; Protein 6g; Carbohydrate 34.3g, of which sugars 34.2g; Fat 22g, of which saturates 13.1g; Cholesterol 150mg; Calcium 182mg; Fibre 1.2g; Sodium 84mg.

CLASSIC TRIPLE CHOCOLATE TERRINE

This variation on Neapolitan ice cream is made with smooth, dark, milk and white chocolate.
It is an impressive dish to serve at dinner parties.

Serves 8–10

6 egg yolks
115g/4oz/generous ½ cup
caster (superfine) sugar
5ml/1 tsp cornflour (cornstarch)
450ml/¾ pint/scant 2 cups
semi-skimmed (low-fat) milk
115g/4oz dark (bittersweet)
chocolate, broken into
squares
115g/4oz milk chocolate,
broken into squares
115g/4oz white chocolate,
broken into squares
2.5ml/½ tsp natural vanilla
extract
450ml/¾ pint/scant 2 cups
whipping cream

Whisk the egg yolks, sugar and cornflour until thick. Pour the milk into a pan and bring to the boil. Pour it on to the yolk mixture, whisking constantly, then return the mixture to the pan and simmer, stirring, until the custard thickens and is smooth.

Divide the custard among three bowls. Add the chocolates: the dark to one, milk to another, and white and vanilla to the third. Stir with separate spoons until the chocolate has melted. Cool, then chill. Line a 25 x 7.5 x 7.5cm/10 x 3 x 3in terrine or large loaf tin (pan) with clear film (plastic wrap).

Stir a third of the cream into each bowl, then churn the milk chocolate custard mixture in an ice cream maker until thick. Return the remaining bowls of flavoured custard and cream mixture to the refrigerator. Spoon the milk chocolate ice cream into the terrine or tin, level the surface and freeze the ice cream until it is firm. If you do not have an ice cream maker thicken each custard mixture in turn by placing it in the freezer for an hour

Churn the white chocolate ice cream until it is thick and smooth, then spoon it into the tin. Level the surface and freeze the ice cream until it is firm. Finally, churn the dark chocolate ice cream and spread it in the tin to form the top layer, smoothing down the surface.

Cover the terrine with clear film, then freeze it overnight. To serve, remove the clear film cover, then invert on to a plate. Peel off the clear film and serve in slices.

Energy 453kcal/1889kJ; Protein 6.6g; Carbohydrate 35.9g, of which sugars 35.8g; Fat 32.5g, of which saturates 18.9g; Cholesterol 174mg; Calcium 160mg; Fibre 0.4g; Sodium 60mg.

WHITE CHOCOLATE AND BROWNIE TORTE

An exceedingly rich dessert, this quick but impressive-looking dish is guaranteed to appeal to chocolate lovers. The great thing about this recipe is that it uses very few ingredients.

Serves 10

300g/11oz white chocolate, broken into pieces
600ml/1 pint/2½ cups double (heavy) cream
250g/9oz rich chocolate brownies
unsweetened cocoa powder, for dusting

COOK'S TIPS
• If you are unable to find good quality brownies, use a moist chocolate sponge instead.
• Serve with a fresh fruit salad as a foil to the richness, topped with a purée made from lightly cooked raspberries.

Energy 570kcal/2365kJ; Protein 5.2g; Carbohydrate 31.1g, of which sugars 25.7g; Fat 48.1g, of which saturates 25.6g; Cholesterol 82mg; Calcium 129mg; Fibre 0g; Sodium 154mg.

Dampen the sides of a 20cm/8in springform tin (pan) and line with a strip of baking parchment. Put the chocolate in a small pan. Add 150ml/¼ pint/⅔ cup of the cream and heat very gently until the chocolate has melted. Stir until smooth, then pour into a bowl and leave to cool.

Break the chocolate brownies into chunky pieces and sprinkle these on the bottom of the prepared tin. Pack them down lightly to make a fairly dense base.

Whip the remaining cream until it forms soft peaks, then fold in the white chocolate mixture.

Spoon into the tin to cover the layer of brownies, then tap the tin gently on the work surface to level the chocolate mixture. Cover the tin and freeze for a few hours or overnight.

Transfer the torte to the refrigerator about 45 minutes before serving. Remove the tin, dust with cocoa powder and enjoy.

CHOCOLATE CANDIES AND SWEET TREATS

WHETHER YOU MAKE THEM AS GIFTS OR AS
TREATS FOR YOURSELF, HAND-MADE CHOCOLATES
AND CANDIES ARE FABULOUS. FROM HAZELNUT
FUDGE TO CHOCOLATE CHERRY WEDGES THESE
SWEET DELIGHTS ARE SURE TO HIT THE SPOT.

WHITE CHOCOLATE SNOWBALLS

These little spherical cookies are particularly popular during the Christmas season. They're simple to make, yet utterly delicious and bursting with creamy, buttery flavours.

Makes 16

200g/7oz white chocolate
25g/1oz/2 tbsp butter, diced
90g/3½oz/generous 1 cup
    desiccated (dry unsweetened
    shredded) coconut
90g/3½oz plain sponge or
    Madeira cake
icing (confectioners') sugar,
    for dusting

> **COOK'S TIP**
> Be prepared to shape the mixture into balls as soon as you've mixed in the desiccated coconut and the cake. The mixture will set extremely quickly and you won't be able to shape it once it has hardened.

Energy 133kcal/554kJ; Protein 1.6g;
Carbohydrate 10.9g, of which sugars 9.7g;
Fat 9.5g, of which saturates 6.6g;
Cholesterol 3mg; Calcium 38mg;
Fibre 0.8g; Sodium 46mg.

Break the chocolate into pieces and put in a heatproof bowl with the butter. Rest the bowl over a pan of gently simmering water and stir frequently until melted. Remove the bowl from the heat and set aside for a few minutes.

Meanwhile, put 50g/2oz/⅔ cup of the desiccated coconut on a plate and set aside.

Crumble the sponge or Madeira cake and add to the melted chocolate with the remaining coconut. Mix well to form a chunky paste.

Take spoonfuls of the mixture and roll into balls, about 2.5cm/1in in diameter, and immediately roll them in the reserved coconut. Place the balls on baking parchment and leave to set.

Before serving, dust the snowballs liberally with plenty of icing sugar.

CHOCOLATE RASPBERRY MELTAWAYS

These soft, velvety meltaways are made with a fruity, fresh raspberry purée that brings out the flavour of the dark chocolate and would make an ideal gift.

Makes 50–100

115g/4oz coconut oil
400g/14oz dark (bittersweet)
    chocolate (at least 60%
    cocoa solids), chopped
100g/3¾oz/1¼ cups puréed
    raspberries, strained
250g/9oz dark chocolate (at
    least 60% cocoa solids),
    tempered (see page 10)
100g/3¾oz milk chocolate,
    tempered (see page 10)
edible pink dust or silver balls

COOK'S TIP
Serve immediately or store in an airtight container, spaced apart, in the refrigerator. Remove 30 minutes before serving to reach room temperature.

Energy 49kcal/204kJ; Protein 0g;
Carbohydrate 5g, of which sugars 5g; Fat
3g, of which saturates 2g; Cholesterol 1mg;
Calcium 5mg; Fibre 0g; Sodium 1mg

Line a 15cm/6in or 20cm/8in square cake tin (pan) with baking parchment. Melt the coconut oil very gently in a large heatproof bowl positioned over a pan of simmering water. Use a sugar thermometer to ensure that it does not rise above 24°C/74°F.

Whisk in the chopped chocolate until smooth. Stir in the raspberry purée. Pour the mixture into the tin. Chill for 30 minutes, until set.

Turn the set mixture out on to a marble slab or other cold, hard surface. Dip a knife in hot water, wipe it dry and use it to slice the block into 2cm/¾in squares. Chill the pieces again for 10 minutes.

Temper the remaining dark chocolate. Dip the raspberry pieces into the tempered chocolate and transfer to a sheet of baking parchment.

Decorate with a drizzle of tempered milk chocolate and sprinkle the tops with edible pink dust, or add silver balls.

EASY CHOCOLATE HAZELNUT FUDGE

You can ring the changes with this scrumptious fudge by making a second batch using white chocolate. Pour this on top of the first (after it's set) to make two-tone fudge.

Makes 16 squares

150ml/¼ pint/⅔ cup evaporated milk
350g/12oz/1½ cups caster (superfine) sugar
large pinch of salt
50g/2oz/½ cup hazelnuts, halved
350g/12oz/2 cups plain (semisweet) chocolate chips

Generously grease a 20cm/8in square cake tin (pan).

Place the evaporated milk, sugar and salt in a heavy pan. Bring to the boil over a medium heat, stirring constantly. Lower the heat and simmer gently, stirring, for 5 minutes.

Remove from the heat and add the hazelnuts and chocolate chips. Stir until the chocolate has melted.

Quickly pour the fudge mixture into the prepared tin and spread evenly. Leave to cool and set.

When the chocolate hazelnut fudge has set, use a sharp knife to cut it into 2.5cm/1in squares.

Store the fudge squares in a large airtight container in a cool place, separating the layers of fudge with baking parchment.

Energy 231kcal/975kJ; Protein 2.4g;
Carbohydrate 38.3g, of which sugars 38g;
Fat 8.7g, of which saturates 4.2g;
Cholesterol 3mg; Calcium 48mg;
Fibre 0.8g; Sodium 14mg.

ALMOND-SCENTED CHOCOLATE CHERRY WEDGES

These cookies are a chocoholic's dream, and use the very best quality chocolate. Erratically shaped,
they are packed with crunchy cookies, juicy raisins and munchy nuts.

Makes about 15

50g/2oz ratafia biscuits (almond
   macaroons) or small amaretti
90g/3½oz shortcake cookies
150g/5oz/1 cup jumbo raisins
50g/2oz/¼ cup undyed glacé
   (candied) cherries, quartered
450g/1lb dark (bittersweet)
   chocolate (minimum
   70 per cent cocoa solids)
90g/3½oz/7 tbsp unsalted
   (sweet) butter, diced
30ml/2 tbsp amaretto liqueur
   (optional)
25g/1oz/¼ cup toasted flaked
   (sliced) almonds

Line a baking sheet with baking parchment. Put the ratafia biscuits or amaretti in a large bowl. Leave half whole and break the remainder into coarse pieces. Break each of the shortcake biscuits into three or four jagged pieces and add to the bowl. Add the raisins and cherries and toss lightly together.

Melt the chocolate and butter with the liqueur, if using, in a heatproof bowl over a pan of hot water. When melted, remove from the heat and stir until combined. Set aside to cool slightly.

Pour the chocolate over the biscuit mixture and stir together until combined. Spread out over the prepared baking sheet. Sprinkle over the almonds and push them in at angles so they stick well to the chocolate-coated biscuits.

When the mixture is cold and set, cut or break into crazy shapes, such as long thin triangles or short stumpy squares.

Energy 288kcal/1206kJ; Protein 2.7g; Carbohydrate 34.6g, of which sugars 29.7g; Fat 16.4g, of which saturates 9.5g; Cholesterol 20mg; Calcium 31mg; Fibre 1.3g; Sodium 75mg.

TRIPLE CHOCOLATE BROWNIE POPS

Rich, indulgent brownie pops are perfect for any occasion – dipped in melted white chocolate and decorated with brightly coloured sugar sprinkles, children in particular will love them.

Makes 24

For the brownies

250g/9oz/generous 1 cup unsalted (sweet) butter

350g/12oz plain (semisweet) chocolate, roughly chopped

250g/9oz/scant 1⅓ cups caster (superfine) sugar

250g/9oz/generous 1 cup soft dark brown sugar

5 eggs

5ml/1 tsp vanilla extract

200g/7oz/1¾ cups plain (all-purpose) flour, sifted

200g/7oz white chocolate chips

To decorate and serve

24 lollipop sticks

150g/5oz white chocolate, coloured sugar sprinkles and chocolate sprinkles

Preheat the oven to 180°C/350°F/Gas 4. Grease and line a 30 x 20cm/ 12 x 8in deep baking tin (pan).

For the brownies, put the butter and plain chocolate in a heatproof bowl set over a pan of simmering water. Stir until melted and combined. Remove from the heat and leave to cool.

Using an electric hand mixer or whisk, whisk the caster sugar, brown sugar, eggs and vanilla extract in a large bowl until the mixture is very light and has doubled in volume. While you continue to whisk, slowly pour in the cooled melted chocolate mixture, whisking until fully incorporated.

Sift in the flour and fold into the chocolate mixture with the chocolate chips. Pour the brownie mixture (batter) into the tin.

Bake for 25–35 minutes, or until it has formed a crust and the tip of a sharp knife inserted into the centre comes out clean. Leave the brownie to cool completely in the tin. Once cool, turn out on to a clean work surface or board.

Cut out 24 rounds of brownie using a 5cm/2in round cutter.

Insert a stick into each brownie. To decorate, melt the white chocolate in a heatproof bowl set over a pan of simmering water. Dip each brownie pop into the melted white chocolate, then decorate with sprinkles and leave to set before serving.

Energy 295kcal/1235kJ; Protein 4g; Carbohydrate 33g, of which sugars 26g; Fat 17g, of which saturates 10g; Cholesterol 72mg; Calcium 65mg; Fibre 0.3g; Sodium 58mg.

COFFEE CHOCOLATE TRUFFLES

A treat for yourself or to give as gifts, these truffles are deceptively easy to make. Because they contain fresh cream, they should be stored in the refrigerator and eaten within a few days.

Makes 24

350g/12oz plain
   (semisweet) chocolate
75ml/5 tbsp double (heavy)
   cream
30ml/2 tbsp coffee liqueur,
   such as Tia Maria, Kahlúa
   or Toussaint
115g/4oz white chocolate
115g/4oz milk chocolate

Energy 138kcal/575kJ; Protein 2g;
Carbohydrate 13g, of which sugars 13g;
Fat 9g, of which saturates 4g;
Cholesterol 2mg; Calcium 21mg;
Fibre 0g; Sodium 47mg

Melt 225g/8oz of the plain chocolate in a bowl over a pan of barely simmering water. Stir in the cream and liqueur, then chill the mixture in the refrigerator for 4 hours, until firm.

Divide the mixture into 24 equal pieces and quickly roll each into a ball. Chill for one more hour, or until they are firm again.

Melt the remaining plain, white and milk chocolate in separate small bowls. Using two forks, carefully dip eight of the truffles, one at a time, into the melted milk chocolate.

Repeat with the white and plain chocolate. Place the truffles on a board, covered with baking parchment and place in the refrigerator. Leave to set before removing and placing in a serving bowl or in individual paper cases.

REAL HOT CHOCOLATE

There are few better ways to enjoy the pleasures of chocolate than with a warming mug of proper hot chocolate. If you want a more chocolatey flavour, then simply increase the amount of chocolate.

Serves 2

*115g/4oz plain (semisweet)
    chocolate with more than
    60 per cent cocoa solids
400ml/14fl oz/1²/₃ cups milk*

COOK'S TIP
This is the essence of real hot chocolate. The powdered version that comes in a packet doesn't even compare. Try to make it with the best chocolate you can afford – you'll really notice the difference. This is how the Spanish and Mexicans have been making hot chocolate for centuries, and it's pure heaven.

Energy 386kcal/1619kJ; Protein 9.7g;
Carbohydrate 45.9g, of which sugars 45.4g;
Fat 19.5g, of which saturates 11.8g;
Cholesterol 15mg; Calcium 259mg;
Fibre 1.5g; Sodium 90mg.

Break up the chocolate and put it in a heatproof bowl or double boiler set over a pan of barely simmering water.

Leave the chocolate in the bowl for 10 minutes until it has completely melted and is smooth.

Add the milk to a small pan and, over a medium heat, bring it just to a boil.

Stir a little of the hot milk into the melted chocolate.

Whisk in the remaining milk – a hand-held blender is good for this – until frothy.

Pour the hot chocolate into mugs and drink while warm.

INDEX

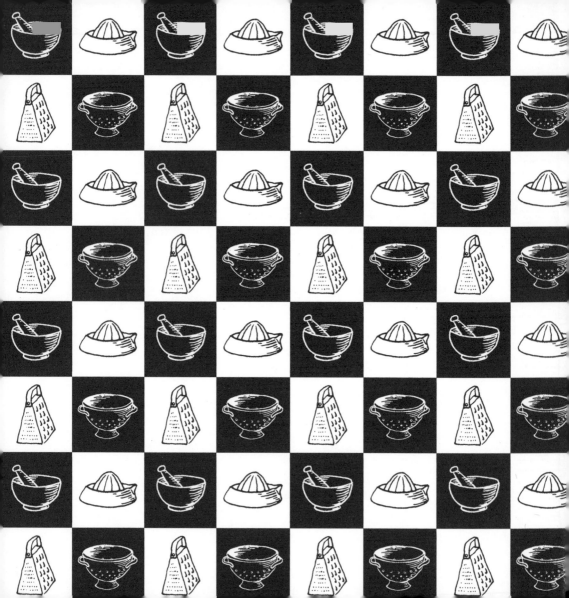